DUDLEY SCHOOLS
LIBRARY SERVICE

D1642389

Schools Library and Information Services

S00000722512

Sewers
and Gutters

Sharon Katz Cooper

www.raintreepublishers.co.uk
Visit our website to find out
more information about
Raintree books.

To order:
☎ Phone +44 (0) 1865 888066
🖨 Fax +44 (0) 1865 314091
💻 Visit www.raintreepublishers.co.uk

Raintree is an imprint of Capstone Global Library Limited,
a company incorporated in England and Wales having its
registered office at 7 Pilgrim Street, London, EC4V 6LB
– Registered company number: 6695582

"Raintree" is a registered trademark of Pearson Education
Limited, under licence to Capstone Global Library Limited

Text © Capstone Global Library Limited 2010
First published in hardback in 2010

The moral rights of the proprietor have been asserted.

All rights reserved. No part of this publication may be
reproduced in any form or by any means (including
photocopying or storing it in any medium by electronic
means and whether or not transiently or incidentally to
some other use of this publication) without the written
permission of the copyright owner, except in accordance
with the provisions of the Copyright, Designs, and Patents
Act 1988 or under the terms of a licence issued by the
Copyright Licensing Agency, Saffron House, 6–10 Kirby
Street, London EC1N 8TS (www.cla.co.uk). Applications
for the copyright owner's written permission should be
addressed to the publisher.

Edited by Charlotte Guillain, Rebecca Rissman,
and Siân Smith
Designed by Joanna Hinton-Malivoire
Picture research by Tracy Cummins and Heather Mauldin
Originated by Chroma Graphics (Overseas) Pte. Ltd
Printed and bound in China by Leo Paper Products

ISBN 978 1 406212 89 1 (hardback)
14 13 12 11 10
10 9 8 7 6 5 4 3 2 1

British Library Cataloguing in Publication Data
Katz Cooper, Sharon.
Sewers and gutters. -- (Horrible habitats)
577.5'5-dc22
A full catalogue record for this book is available from the
British Library.

Acknowledgements
The author and publisher are grateful to the following
for permission to reproduce copyright material: Age
Fotostock p. **16** (© Bildagentur Waldhaeusl/waldhaeusl
com); Alamy pp. **4** (© Arco Images GmbH), **7** (© Mike
Rinnan), **11** (© Mike Lane), **26** (© Ashley Cooper);
Animals Animals p. **13** (© Mickey Gibson); Ardea p. **8**
(© John Daniels); DRK Photo p. **29** (© William P. Leonard);
Dwight Kuhn Photography pp. **14**, **15** (© Dave Kuhn);
Getty Images pp. **5** (© Bert Klassen), **19** (© Joe Raedle/
Staff); Minden p. **10** (© Stephen Dalton); National
Geographic Stock p. **9** (© James L. Stanfield); Nature
Picture Library pp. **20** (© Phil Savoie), **23** (© Jane Burton);
Photolibrary pp. **6** (© Photononstop/Jacques Loic), **12**
(© Bartomeu Borrell), **24** (© Mike Anich); Photo
Researchers, Inc. p. **21** (© Dr. Merlin D. Tuttle/Bat
Conservation International); Shutterstock pp. **17** (© Mau
Horng), **18** (© Saniphoto), **22** (© Christopher Tan Teck
Hean), **25** (© Steve McWilliam), **27** (© Timothy Large).

Cover photograph of a rat reproduced with permission of
Ardea (© John Daniels).

Every effort has been made to contact copyright holders
of material reproduced in this book. Any omissions will
be rectified in subsequent printings if notice is given to
the publishers.

Disclaimer
All the Internet addresses (URLs) given in this book were valid
at the time of going to press. However, due to the dynamic
nature of the Internet, some addresses may have changed, or
sites may have changed or ceased to exist since publication.
While the author and publishers regret any inconvenience
this may cause readers, no responsibility for any such changes
can be accepted by either the author or the publishers.

Some words are shown in bold, **like this**. You can find
out what they mean by looking in the glossary.

Contents

DUDLEY PUBLIC LIBRARIES

L

722512   SCH

J 574.5

What is a habitat?

A **habitat** is a place where plants and animals can find what they need to live. What are those needs? Plants and animals need food, water, and shelter.

rat

4

Almost any place can be a **habitat**. You can find **sewers** under the streets. Sewers are filled with the dirty water from streets, houses, and toilets.

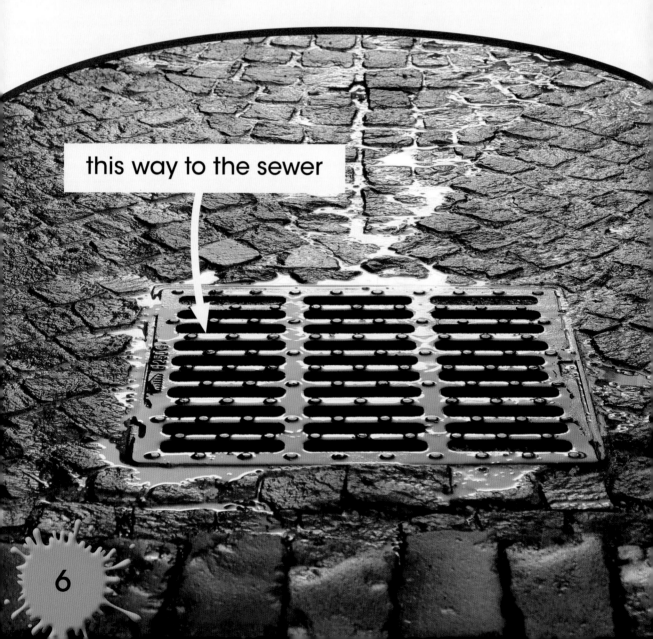

this way to the sewer

What could you
find living in the
dirty water and rotting
leaves in this gutter?

A **gutter** is the tube that catches
leaves and water from the roofs of
houses. Even sewers and gutters
are habitats!

Rats all around

Rats live everywhere people do. There are thousands and even millions of them in city **sewers**. Why? They can find lots of water and food down there.

Norway rat

These hungry rats are searching for food.

nest

Rats often build their nests in places connected to **sewers**. They go into the sewer to find food.

10

FUN FACT

Some of a rat's favourite foods are human poo and ground-up food from kitchen sinks. They also like to eat dead rats and cockroaches.

Cockroaches are easy to find in **sewers**. They feed on dead and rotting plants and animals. That is exactly what they find down there. They also like to be in the dark, and it is always dark in the sewers!

These cockroaches are enjoying rotting kiwi fruit.

13

Cockroaches need to drink. They sometimes get water from toilets and dirty puddles. This is one reason they spread dirt and carry **diseases**.

Lots of poo can be found in sewers. This cockroach is eating some!

poo ⟶

Cockroaches are insects. They have six legs and run very fast. They leave behind a trail of smelly, oily liquid. Other cockroaches like the smell and come running.

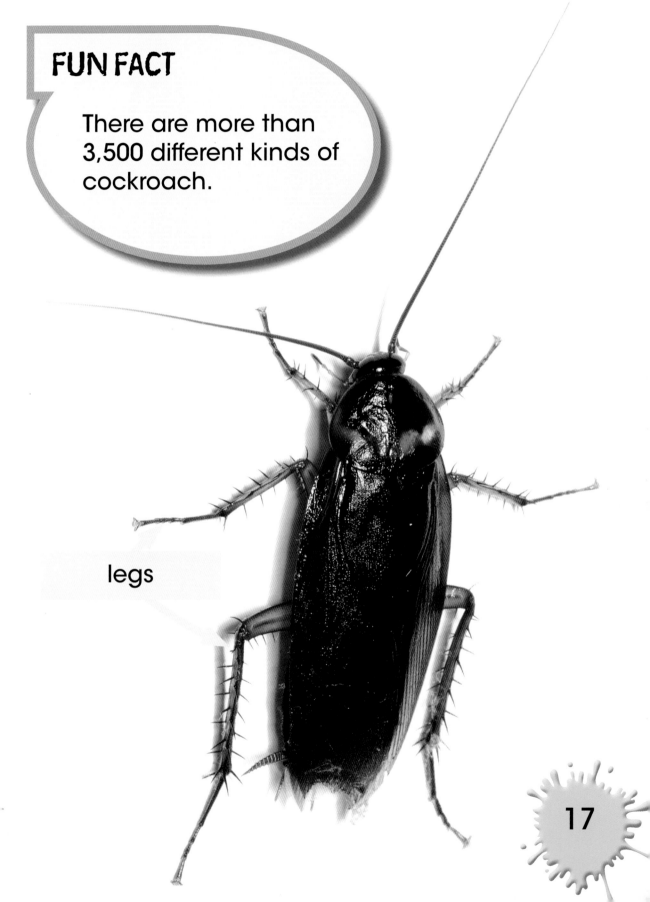

FUN FACT

There are more than 3,500 different kinds of cockroach.

legs

17

Sewer surprises

Some people have unkindly flushed baby alligators down the toilet in the past. Anything that is flushed down a toilet travels to the **sewers**.

baby alligator

FUN FACT

Alligators have been found in sewers. Young alligators might be able to live in a sewer for a while by eating rats. It is unlikely that any fully grown alligators could be found in sewers today, though.

19

Big brown bats

Brown bats sometimes sleep for the winter in **sewers** and other dark underground places. This is called **hibernation**. They even sleep in graveyards.

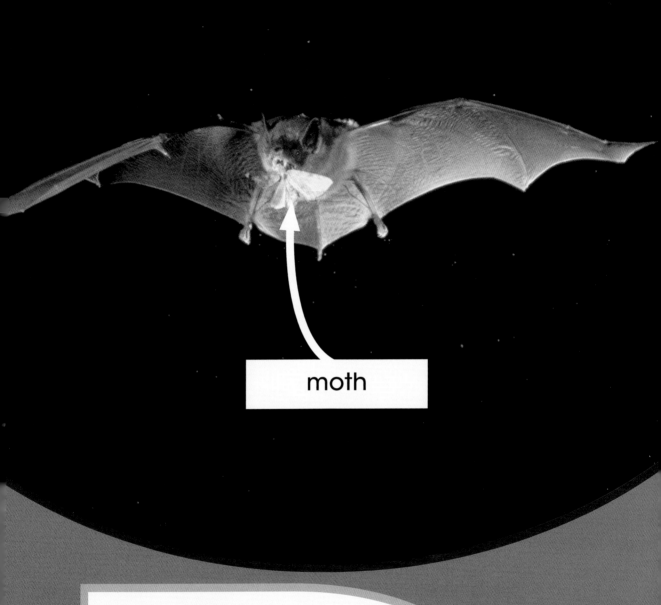

moth

FUN FACT

Brown bats fly out at night
to look for insects to eat.
They eat mosquitoes,
beetles, and moths.

Slimy snails and slugs

You may find snails moving slowly around **gutters**. Snails' bodies make a lot of slime. This slime is so thick that it acts like a suction cup. The suction helps snails travel upside down!

Snails move by creeping along on a flat foot underneath their bodies. Unlike us, snails only have one foot!

Snails can't hear but they can feel vibrations.

23

Gutters also attract slugs. This is because slugs like to eat rotting plants and leaves. Just like snails, slugs are covered with a slime called **mucus**. Mucus keeps their skins **moist**, or slightly wet.

FUN FACT

Slug bodies are often covered with mites. Mites are tiny creatures that will bite into a slug's skin and suck its blood.

Slugs trail slime from their undersides.
This slime helps them slide along the
ground. They leave a trail of slime
behind them.

slug trail

FUN FACT

Slugs have holes in the sides of their bodies! A slug takes air into its body through this hole and the hole can open or close.

27

Follow a slug

What you need:
- your eyes
- an area where you can find slugs

What to do:
1. Go outside after it has rained and look around.

2. Find a slug and look for its slime trail.

3. How far back can you trace it? Can you see where it has been? Where do you think it might be going? Can you see the hole in its side?

29

Glossary

disease illness

gutter tube that catches water from the roofs of houses. Many rotting leaves get stuck in gutters, too.

habitat place where animals or plants live and grow

hibernation sleeping for a long time in winter, saving energy

moist slightly wet or damp

mucus slippery stuff that animals produce from their bodies

sewer place under the street where the dirty water from streets and houses goes

Find out more

Find out

Which snails are the fastest?

Books to read

Animal Neighbours: Rat, Stephen Savage (Wayland, 2007)

Bug Books: Cockroach, Karen Hartley, Chris Macro, and Philip Taylor (Heinemann Library, 2008)

Bug Books: Snail, Karen Hartley and Chris Macro (Heinemann Library, 2008)

Websites

http://www.bats.org.uk/pages/batsforkids.html
This website has lots of information about how you can help save bat habitats.

http://www.geocities.com/sseagraves/allaboutsnails.htm
This website is packed with snail facts and activities.

http://www.nhm.ac.uk/kids-only/life/life-small/cockroaches/
Find out some fascinating facts about cockroaches on this website.

31

Index